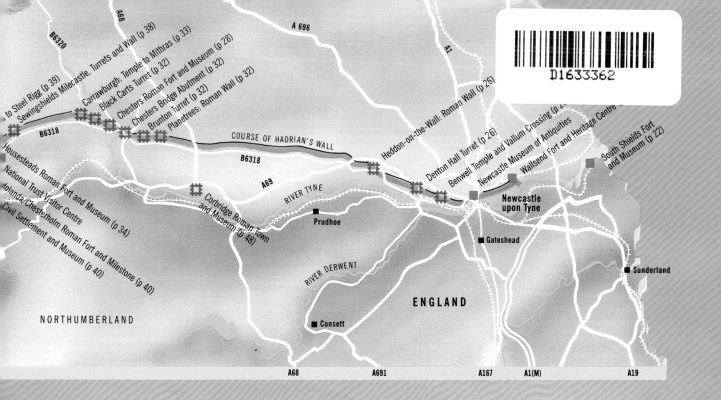

EXPLORING THE WALL
with recommended tours and plans

Published by ENGLISH HERITAGE
Text by David J BREEZE, BA, PhD, FSA
Edited by Ken Osborne and
designed by Martin Atcherley
Copyright © English Heritage, London 1996
First published 1987. Third Edition 1996
ISBN 1 85074 252 9

What is Hadrian's Wall?

Hadrian's Wall is the most important monument built by the Romans in Britain. It is the best known frontier in the entire Roman empire and stands today as a reminder of the past glories of one of the world's greatest empires.

Some 1850 years ago the Roman empire covered much of the then known world. It stretched from north Britain eastwards for 2,500 miles to present-day Iraq and southwards to the Sahara desert 1,500 miles distant. For 300 years Hadrian's Wall was the north-west frontier of that empire.

Roman armies first invaded Britain under Julius Caesar in 55 BC, but permanent conquest only began in AD 43. In that year the Emperor Claudius launched an invasion of the island. Forty years later the Romans defeated the Caledonians at the Battle of Mons Graupius and the conquest of the island seemed complete. Subsequent reverses on the Danube led to troop withdrawals from Britain and thus, shortly after AD 100, the northernmost army units in Britain lay along the Tyne-Solway isthmus. Across the isthmus a road, now known as the Stanegate, provided ready communication between Corbridge and Carlisle, both situated on important north-south routes.

It was on this line in the 120s that the Emperor Hadrian ordered the construction of the Wall which now bears his name. When eventually completed, Hadrian's Wall ran for 80 Roman miles (73 modern miles or 117 km) from Wallsend on the river Tyne to Bowness on the Solway Firth and was of stone throughout its length.

As first planned, Hadrian's Wall was to consist of a stone **wall** running from Newcastle to the river Irthing, a distance of 45 Roman miles. From the Irthing to the Solway the 'wall' was built of turf blocks. This was not an impenetrable barrier, for at mile intervals there were gates, each defended by a small guard post, known today as **milecastles**. Two towers (**turrets**) were placed between each pair of milecastles, for observation, and it is probable that there was

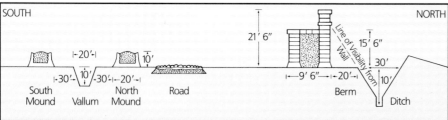

SOUTH — NORTH

South Mound | Vallum | North Mound | Road | Berm | Ditch

21' 6" — Line of visibility from Wall — 15' 6" — 30' — 9' 6" — 20' — 10' — 20' — 10' — 30' — 10' — 30' — 20'

◀ *Diagrammatic section across Hadrian's Wall. The Vallum was generally about 60 to 100 yards behind the Wall, but the distance could vary from a few yards to nearly a mile*

▼ *Reconstruction by Peter Connolly of Hadrian's Wall showing a turret in the foreground and a milecastle beyond. This is but one of several possible reconstructions of Hadrian's Wall*

▲ *A coin of the Emperor Hadrian found in the river Tyne at Newcastle*

▶ *A model of the fort at Benwell in the Museum of Antiquities, Newcastle. The fort lies astride the Wall with three of its four main gates opening north of the Wall. Within the fort walls the buildings are packed close together. The headquarters building in the centre is flanked to the right by the commanding officer's house and to the left by granaries. The other buildings include a hospital, barrack-blocks, stables and store-houses*

▶ *A model of a stone milecastle in the Museum of Antiquities, Newcastle. There are gates to north and south, to allow soldiers and civilians to pass through the Wall. Within the milecastle a barrack-block afforded accommodation for 8 men. At least 2 milecastles seem to have housed 32 men. There may have been a tower over the south gate as well as the north gate of the mile-castle*

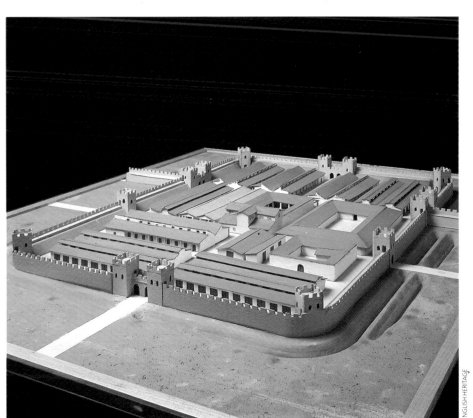

▲ *A free-standing tower on the bank of the river Danube as depicted on Trajan's Column almost contemporary with the building of Hadrian's Wall. Towers on the Wall may have been similar to this*

a tower over the north gate of each milecastle, ensuring an unbroken pattern. The turrets were of stone, on stone and turf walls alike. On the stone wall the milecastles were of stone; on the turf wall they were of turf and timber.

In front of the Wall lay a **ditch**, except where the crags made it superfluous. The material from the ditch was tipped out on to the north side to form an outer mound.

The Wall crossed three main rivers, the North Tyne, the Irthing and the Eden. Here **bridges** were provided to aid lateral communication. Another new bridge was probably built at the time across the Tyne at Newcastle and named *Pons Aelius* (Aelius was Hadrian's family name).

Originally the troops based in the milecastles and turrets were probably drawn from the army units stationed behind the Wall, for at first there was no intention to place complete units on the Wall line itself. These regiments would remain in their existing bases in northern Britain, and the Wall was built as a separate, and additional, element to the frontier. The position of the Stanegate, as well as the geography of the area, thus governed the position of the Wall. It ran along the crags in front of the Stanegate from Sewingshields to Carvoran. To the east of Sewingshields it headed for the vantage point of Limestone Corner and then turned to make for Newcastle. After crossing the North Tyne at

▲ The Wall at Willowford looking east. The wall and ditch are separated by a strip of ground 20 feet wide. The wall was originally planned to be 10 Roman feet (3 m) thick and was perhaps 15 feet (4.6 m) high to a wall-walk. The ditch, usually about 30 feet (10 m) wide and 10 feet (3 m) deep, formerly had a V-shaped profile, here modified to take a modern farm track

Chesters it followed the northern rim of the Tyne Valley. West of Carvoran the Wall crossed the Irthing at Willowford and lay forward of the river until, at Carlisle, the relationship was reversed and for its last 15 miles the Wall ran along behind the Solway.

The system of milecastles and turrets was continued for at least another 26 miles down the **Cumbrian coast** to Maryport. No wall was built here, and, although in some places a fence was constructed, the sea was considered a sufficient barrier.

This first plan for Hadrian's Wall was never completed. While work was still in progress a number of modifications were made. First, it was decided to move some regiments up on to the Wall itself. The new **forts** built at this time lay astride the Wall wherever possible. Secondly, behind the Wall was now constructed the **Vallum**, a great earthwork stretching along the whole length of the frontier from Tyne to Solway. This

probably served as the Roman equivalent of barbed wire, defining the rear of the military zone. Crossings through the Vallum were provided, but only at forts; no provision was made for crossing at milecastles. In order to construct both forts and Vallum, troops were taken off building the wall. When they returned to the wall, its width was reduced from the original 10 Roman feet to 8 feet or less, presumably to speed up progress. This was not the last alteration to be made to Hadrian's Wall. A four-mile extension was constructed down the Tyne from Newcastle to Wallsend, one or two more forts were added including Carrawburgh, and a start was made on rebuilding the turf wall in stone. Later in the century a road, the **Military Way**, was constructed behind the Wall, linking the forts.

Examples of most of the elements of Hadrian's Wall are in the care of English Heritage and are described in this guidebook.

▲ *Aerial view of Hadrian's Wall at Cawfields looking east. Cawfields milecastle lies bottom left and the Wall runs on along the crags. The Vallum, consisting of a ditch with a mound set back on each side, follows the easier ground to the right. Between Wall and Vallum runs the Military Way. Today the landscape is open. In Roman times there would have been more trees, though the hills were probably already bare while farmers would have cleared much of the lower ground for pasture and cereal cultivation*

◀ *This section across the turf wall shows that it was constructed of turf blocks. A Roman military manual laid down that these should measure 18 by 12 by 6 inches. The traces of Roman grass survive as dark lines capping the lighter coloured earth of the turfs. The turf wall was 20 Roman feet (6 m) wide at its base*

Who built Hadrian's Wall?

'Hadrian was the first to build a wall, 80 miles long, to separate the Romans and the barbarians'—*Roman biography of Hadrian*

This is the only reference in ancient literature to the building of Hadrian's Wall. Yet it is most useful for it provides an approximate date for its construction, a statement of its length and a comment on its purpose. It was in 122 that the Emperor Hadrian came to visit Britain, one of the many stops on a tour of the western provinces of the Roman empire, and it was probably during the visit that he ordered the construction of the Wall.

Hadrian did not wish to extend the limits of the empire, but was content to see it prosper within the boundaries he had inherited: indeed he even gave up some of the conquests of his relation and predecessor, the Emperor Trajan. Hadrian appreciated two important facts relevant to the safety of his people: the army must be continually trained so that it was ready to defend the empire at any time, and the construction of artificial frontiers would help prevent disruption of life in the frontier areas by unruly elements beyond. Thus Hadrian spent considerable

▲ *Altar to the Discipline of the Emperors erected at Corbridge and dedicated by soldiers of legion II Augusta*

▲ *Hadrian's tours to inspect the provincial armies of the empire were celebrated by special coin issues. This shows the emperor addressing the army of Britain, which is represented by five soldiers holding standards*

▲ *This scene on Trajan's Column, erected in Rome in 113, shows legionaries cutting logs and turfs to construct a rampart. In the foreground two ditches are being dug and the earth is being removed in baskets. Soldiers in the background are carrying turfs on their shoulders, holding them in place by short lengths of rope. To the right are placed their javelins, helmets and shields, though each soldier retains his sword*

time inspecting the army, supervising its training and improving morale: he also fostered the religious cult of Discipline. At the same time in Germany and in Britain he ordered the construction of two great frontiers.

The construction of Hadrian's Wall was carried out almost entirely by soldiers from the three legions of the province: the Second based at Caerleon near Newport in south Wales, the Sixth from York and the Twentieth stationed at Chester. It is a common fallacy to envisage the Wall being built by slave labour. This was not a practice followed by the Roman army. Within their ranks the legions contained architect-engineers, surveyors, masons, carpenters, and glaziers – in short all

Building tools

Slater's hammer   Nails   Chisel   Mason's hammers

Plumb bob

ENGLISH HERITAGE

▶ *This stone, outside Chesters museum, is from a Roman quarry on Fallowfield Fell about ½ mile (1 km) south of Hadrian's Wall. A mason has carved on it Petra Flavi Carantini, the rock of Flavius Carantinus. The stone for Hadrian's Wall was obtained locally from quarries such as the one where this inscription was found. Building materials – mortar, water and timber as well as stone – would be transported to the Wall in carts or on the backs of mules*

MUSEUM OF ANTIQUITIES (NEWCASTLE)

◀ *This diploma (certificate of privileges) was issued on 17 July 122 to Gemellus, son of Breucus, who had just retired from the ala I Pannoniorum Tampiana. He had been discharged by the previous governor Pompeius Falco, but the diploma was not issued until A. Platorius Nepos had assumed office. This dates the arrival of Nepos very closely. He came to Britain from the province of Lower Germany, where he had previously been governor. Hadrian also travelled from that province to Britain in 122, and the two men may have come together. They may also have brought with them legion VI Victrix to help build the Wall. The diploma, which is now in the British Museum, was found in Pannonia (modern Hungary), where Gemellus went in retirement. The facsimile of a diploma dating to 146 and found at Chesters can be seen in the museum at that site*

MUSEUM OF ANTIQUITIES (NEWCASTLE)

◀ *Inscription, found at milecastle 38, records that it was built for the Emperor Caesar Trajan Hadrian Augustus by legion II Augusta under A. Platorius Nepos, governor. Fragments of similar inscriptions have been found at milecastles 37 and 42*

the skills required for even the most massive building task. Nevertheless it is not impossible that local civilians were drafted in to aid in transporting materials.

The building of Hadrian's Wall was to occupy the legionaries for at least the next six years, and modifications to the Wall were still being carried out at the time of Hadrian's death in 138. As so often happens the scale of the building project grew and thus yet more soldiers were drafted in to help. These included men from auxiliary units, the other main branch of the provincial army, and also from the British fleet.

The construction of Hadrian's Wall would not have been a costly venture for the imperial treasury. The builders were soldiers already employed by the state while the materials were there for the taking, if not actually imperial property. If built by civilian contractors, the cost of the Wall would have been astronomical, perhaps £100 million at today's prices.

▶ *This inscription from a building in the fort at Benwell records that it was built for the Emperor Caesar Trajan Hadrian Augustus, under A. Platorius Nepos, governor, by a detachment of the British fleet*

MUSEUM OF ANTIQUITIES (NEWCASTLE)

7

How did Hadrian's Wall function?

There were two separate elements to Hadrian's Wall. One was the barrier itself, together with the milecastles and turrets. The other was represented by the forts. The function of the barrier, in the words of Hadrian's biographer, was to separate the Romans and the barbarians. The purpose of the regiments stationed in the forts was to protect the province from attack. The distinction between these two roles is emphasised by the first plan for the Wall. In that scheme no regiments were stationed on the barrier itself.

In the early years of the empire the army was kept in major groups poised to move forward and conquer new lands, or to intervene internally to put down revolts.

Gradually, as the empire ceased to expand, regiments were spread along the frontiers and, in areas like Britain where the frontier was short, also across the country behind. Forts were often placed about a day's march, 14 miles or so, apart. Thus the regiments could supervise their own locality, but in the event of an attack on the province, could combine to form a force capable of countering an attack in the field, where the Romans were pre-eminent. In such circumstances mobility was important and a barrier of little help.

Hadrian's Wall had a rather different role: frontier control. We know from other frontiers that barbarians – as the Romans called the people beyond their boundaries – could only enter the empire unarmed,

proceeding under military escort to specified markets, where fees were payable. One function of the Wall was to ensure that these regulations were kept. Another role, no doubt, was to put a stop to the casual disturbances endemic on frontiers, such as small-scale raiding.

▼ *This reconstruction view of Hadrian's Wall at Walltown Crags emphasises the way in which the Wall would have prevented free movement into and out of the province. Sorrell's drawing shows a patrol walk along the top of the Wall, but there is no certainty that this existed. The German frontier, built at the same time as Hadrian's Wall, was a fence and thus was not topped by a patrol walk*

Hadrian's Wall did not operate like a medieval town wall: the two were designed to serve different ends. The medieval town wall protected a community of people within a defended circuit. Hadrian's Wall ran for 73 miles across open country serving as a demarcation line. There is no evidence that there was a patrol walk along its top – some Roman frontiers were merely fences and so could not be patrolled in this way. In any case Roman soldiers, unlike their medieval successors, were not best equipped to fight defensively from the top of the walls. Indeed there were not enough soldiers available to man the Wall in sufficient numbers to defend it adequately from an enemy which might attack in strength at any one point.

Hadrian's Wall and the army of the north were but two elements in the protection of the province. In later years the existence of Roman army scouts patrolling north of the Wall is recorded and it seems possible that some surveillance was carried out from the time of the Wall's construction. Rome often concluded treaties with the tribes beyond her boundaries. Towards the end of the second century the long arm of Roman diplomacy stretched over 100 miles (160 km) beyond the Wall to the Caledonians with whom the Romans concluded a treaty, and this may not have been the first. Such relationships were sometimes strengthened through the payment of subsidies. Rome was well versed in the diplomatic as well as the martial arts.

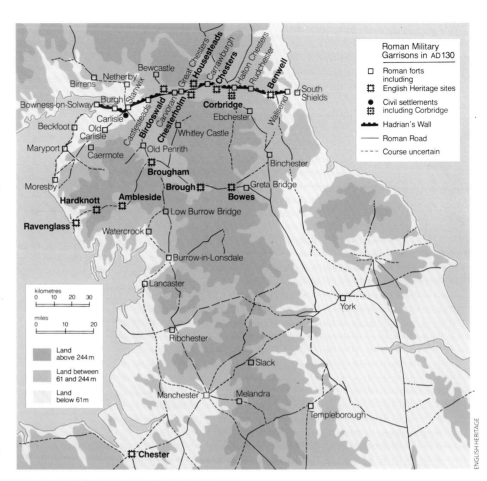

ENGLISH HERITAGE

▲ *North Britain in the time of Hadrian*

◀ *This hoard of nearly 2000 silver denarii was buried at Falkirk near to the abandoned Antonine Wall in or soon after 235. The hoard may have been formed from subsidies paid by the Romans to local chiefs*

▼ *The Ermine Street Guard, a modern reconstruction society, display their auxiliary uniforms*

NATIONAL MUSEUM OF ANTIQUITIES OF SCOTLAND

ENGLISH HERITAGE

Who manned Hadrian's Wall?

The most persistent myth about Hadrian's Wall is that it was guarded by soldiers from Rome or Italy. In fact the troops based in the forts and milecastles of the Wall were mostly recruited from the north-western provinces of the Roman empire. The units might have exotic names, such as *ala I Pannoniorum* which had originally been raised in Pannonia (modern Hungary) or *cohors I Thracum* from Thrace (modern Bulgaria), but once posted to Britain the regiments started recruiting locally. Thus, by the time of Hadrian, many soldiers stationed on the Wall would have been British. Nevertheless the army of Britain continued to receive some recruits from the Continent and throughout the history of the province there were always a number of Gauls and Germans, for example, serving in the island.

Although mainly built by legionaries, the Wall was manned by auxiliaries. These were the second line troops of the Roman army and their name literally meant 'helpers'. Each fort on the Wall appears to have been built to hold a single auxiliary unit. There

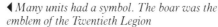

▲ *Auxiliary infantryman (right) and cavalryman of the time of Hadrian; drawn by Peter Connolly*

◀ *Many units had a symbol. The boar was the emblem of the Twentieth Legion*

▼ *The tombstone of an archer in an unknown regiment from Housesteads*

were six different sizes and types of auxiliary regiments and all are attested on the Wall. The most common type of unit was the 500-strong mixed infantry and cavalry regiment. This appears to have been the multi-purpose unit of the Roman army. The 500-strong infantry regiment was also well represented.

There were no legions based nearby, but to compensate for their absence several of the larger cohorts of 1000 men, of both mixed and purely infantry types, were stationed in the Wall area. These regiments were the largest units in the Roman army after the legions.

Cavalry regiments were comparatively rare on Hadrian's Wall and perhaps this reflects the variety of functions which the Wall units had to perform. Nevertheless the only British example of the most prestigious type of auxiliary unit, the 1000-strong cavalry regiment was based on the Wall, at Stanwix near Carlisle. Its commanding officer was the highest ranking officer on the Wall line, but that does not imply that he had any special

authority over the other commanding officers on the frontier. There is no evidence for any local command hierarchy and it is not known what part the legionary legate at York played in the command structure. It seems highly probable nevertheless that some system existed for co-ordination and combination of units.

The commanding officers of auxiliary units were drawn from the gentry and aristocracy of the empire. They came to their first appointments with little if any military experience, and many did not receive further appointments. These men moved freely about the empire commanding regiments and a few rose to the very pinnacle of the imperial civil service.

Infantry units were divided into *centuriae* (centuries), each probably 80 strong (the old link to 100 had long been lost), while the cavalry were subdivided into troops, each probably containing 32 men. The infantry were led by centurions, the cavalry by decurions. These officers had generally risen from the ranks and they formed a professional officer core to the army. They also provided continuity since the commanding officers were career postings, each usually held for three to four years. Each centurion and decurion normally would have had at least 15 years service in the ranks. A few, however, were appointed to their posts directly from civilian life. Centurions and decurions might have continued in harness for decades: the longest known tenure of office by a legionary centurion is 61 years.

Military life on the Wall

There is no contemporary evidence to illustrate daily life on Hadrian's Wall. We do not know how long particular duties lasted or what sort of distances were covered by soldiers on patrol. Nevertheless, on the basis of evidence from other parts of the Roman empire, we can say something about life on the Wall.

The soldier's day started with breakfast. This may have been something like our porridge. The main meal of the day was in the evening. The Roman soldier had a varied diet, eating bread, soup, meat, fish, fruit and vegetables, and drinking beer and cheap wine.

Part of the day might be given over to training. Roman military manuals stressed that all soldiers should receive regular weapons drill, physical training and should participate in military exercises. Special cavalry exercises included mock battles: those performed by the Roman army in Africa in 128 were observed by the Emperor Hadrian.

Many soldiers would be occupied for at least part of the day by fatigues. These included guard duty, cleaning the centurion's uniform and looking after the bath-house. All such tasks were recorded both on duty rosters and on soldiers' files: in the Roman army even horses had their own records while

This purse and its contents of 28 denarii were lost during the building of the fort at Birdoswald. They are presumably the savings of a soldier. The legionary in Hadrian's day was paid 300 denarii a year and the auxiliary infantryman 100 denarii, though both were subject to compulsory deductions for arms and armour, clothing, bedding and food

receipts had to be completed in quadruplicate! Some soldiers had special jobs in the building and maintenance staff or in the regimental office; others were adjutants, standard bearers, or buglers who sounded the watch and indicated orders on the march.

There would have always been some soldiers on duty – or ill – at the fort but many would have been serving elsewhere. Supplies in transit needed protecting while some regiments sent men to serve on the governor's staff in London. The main activity, however, was probably patrolling, either along the Wall or in the lands to the north. Surveillance would have been maintained over the tribes beyond the frontier, many probably being in treaty relationship with Rome. We know from other frontiers that treaties might strictly define the time and place of a tribe's asssembly and that it should be supervised by a Roman officer. Such activities might have taken soldiers far beyond the Wall.

▼ *Recruits training outside a fort; drawn by Peter Connolly*

Food and cooking

▶ *This bronze corn-measure was found at Carvoran. It was once inscribed with the name of the Emperor Domitian, later erased, a weight of 38 pounds, and the dry volume of the contents, 17½ sextarii (about 2 gallons). The writer Polybius recorded that the daily grain ration of each soldier was 2½ sextarii, so it is possible that this measure contained a soldier's weekly ration of grain. If this interpretation is correct, this would be a very early instance of official use of the seven-day week*

◀ *This corn mill, found at Chesters, would have been used by soldiers to grind their daily ration of grain: the handle is modern. Food could be cooked on hearths or in ovens placed at the back of fort walls*

▲ *These two ovens were built on the ground floor of the east tower of the south gate at Birdoswald*

▶ *Model of granary. It is not known whether the grain was stored in bins, as suggested here, or sacks*

Samian cup, made in Gaul (France)

These bowls were made in Britain and were found at Corbridge

Beaker

Cooking pot

The soldier's personal life

Every army has its camp followers. They followed Caesar round Gaul, and others no doubt arrived in Britain in the wake of Claudius's army in AD 43. As the army moved north it was presumably accompanied by various civilians who set up house outside the new forts.

One important group in the civil settlement would have been the soldiers' wives and families. A Roman soldier was not allowed to marry, but there was nothing to stop him from contracting a union with a woman according to local law, and such 'marriages' were subsequently recognised in Roman law when the soldier retired, and his children were legitimised.

The Roman soldier was relatively well paid, and he attracted people who wanted to part him from his money. These included merchants selling food and wine, clothing, pottery and knick-knacks.

Another element in the village was provided by the temples and shrines. Each settlement would have contained a number of temples dedicated to different gods: Roman, local, those brought in by the regiment or other travellers and, in later years, the gods of Eastern mystery religions such as Mithraism.

▶ *In the third century a flourishing civil settlement grew up outside the fort at Housesteads. This reconstruction by Alan and Richard Sorrell is looking up the main street towards the south gate of the fort with half-timbered houses on either side*

ENGLISH HERITAGE

ENGLISH HERITAGE

MUSEUM OF ANTIQUITIES (NEWCASTLE)

▲ *The Rudge Cup dates from the second century. Above what may be a depiction of Hadrian's Wall is a list of the forts in the western half of the Wall. This was presumably one of two or three vessels naming all the forts along the frontier. They were probably made to be sold as souvenirs*

◀ *A gaming board, dice and counters, all found at Corbridge*

MUSEUM OF ANTIQUITIES (NEWCASTLE)

ENGLISH HERITAGE

▲ *A head of the god Hercules found at Housesteads: this would have once adorned a temple*

An arch from the temple of Mars Thincsus at ▲ Housesteads. The German soldiers who worshipped here equated the Roman god of war with their own warlike god Thincsus, who is shown here with his two attendants Beda and Fimmilena (the Alaisiagae). The temple lay on the low hill between the fort and the modern car park

ENGLISH HERITAGE

Beyond the village lay the cemeteries; Roman law forbade burial within built-up areas.

There was no such thing as the week-end or the 48-hour pass in the Roman army. Soldiers had to apply to their centurions for leave and frequently bribed them to obtain it. We do not know how often leave might be obtained. Similarly we know nothing about the number of hours a soldier might be expected to work each day. We do know that there were a number of religious festivals throughout the year – perhaps 50 in total – and these may have been treated as holidays.

It may be suspected that in general the soldiers would try to get away with doing the least possible work. This natural state of affairs was exacerbated by the perennial problem of the peace-time army: as it was not fighting, it had little to do. When Corbulo took over the army of Syria he found, according to Tacitus, that it contained soldiers who had never been on guard duty and did not possess armour. Hadrian, his biographer tells us, demolished dining rooms, covered galleries and ornamentai gardens in forts. Good emperors and generals, such as Hadrian, tried to compensate for this inactivity by training and manoeuvres. Nevertheless it would not be surprising if the civil settlement was as much a home to the soldier as the fort itself.

14

▲ *This altar found at Housesteads, together with the arch above, neatly demonstrates the all-embracing nature of Roman religion being dedicated to the Roman god Mars, the German goddesses Alaisiagae and to the deity of the Emperor by German soldiers in the Frisian unit at Housesteads*

The head of a Celtic horned god found at the ▲ outpost fort at Netherby

▲ *Each of these gods wears the cucullus, a local cloak rather like a duffle coat but without sleeves. The sculpture can be seen in Housesteads museum*

▲ *These two silver plaques were dedicated to the god Cocidius, a local version of Mars. They were found in the strong room of the headquarters building at Bewcastle*

How did the Wall affect the local people?

Contemporary written sources for Hadrian's Wall are scarce, and they tell us nothing about the local people whose lives were affected by this massive building project. Archaeology, however, seems to provide positive evidence for one result of the construction of the Wall. At Milking Gap, 1 mile west of Housesteads, between the Wall and the Vallum, a farmstead was abandoned at about the time the Wall was constructed, probably because it now lay within the military zone: here the hand of the army may be suspected.

The Wall would have had an effect on farming rather similar to a modern motorway, which slices through farmland, destroying old access routes and cutting off fields from the farmsteads. Possibly the Knag Burn gate at Housesteads was broken through the Wall in the fourth century to provide ease of movement for farmers and their beasts.

Hadrian's Wall followed the most convenient geographical and strategic line. It

▲ The Knag Burn gate at Housesteads. Access was through a narrow passage, which had doors at both ends and was flanked by a guard chamber on each side

seems to have ignored local tribal boundaries. At its east end we do not know where the boundary between the Brigantes to the south and the Votadini to the north ran, but it seems unlikely that this was on the line of the Wall, or even the river Tyne to the south. Further west, it seems probable that some Brigantes living on the northern shore of the Solway were cut off from their fellow tribesmen by the construction of the Wall. The outpost forts at Bewcastle, Netherby and Birrens may have been built to protect these people, who were still part of the province, although beyond the Wall.

The building of Hadrian's Wall increased the number of troops based in this part of Britain. The soldiers required feeding and the army preferred to obtain its supplies locally. Thus it might be expected that the arrival of the Roman army in northern Britain in the late first century, and then its strengthening under Hadrian, would lead to

changes in local farming patterns and particularly increased cereal production. There is some archaeological evidence to support this assumption, but unfortunately there has been insufficient work in this field of research to quantify any change.

One major change brought about by the presence of so many Roman soldiers on the Wall was the growth of the settlements outside forts. As well as the soldiers' families and merchants these may also have attracted farmers from the northern countryside: the army probably attracted local boys too as recruits. No evidence for either survives, though a Brigantian is known serving on the Antonine Wall. Certainly, Roman objects found on native settlements and native objects in Roman forts demonstrate some contact between soldier and civilian but the nature of this is unclear.

Rome would have imposed peace (and taxation) on the north, putting an end to the ritualised warfare so beloved of the Celts. This peace would have extended well beyond the Wall into the areas under Roman surveillance. The presence of the army was not wholly advantageous to the local people. Numerous contemporary documents from other parts of the empire record the rapacious activities of Roman soldiers. Other documents show that while the army might have brought peace it could not wholly eradicate brigandage. Dealing with such activities fell to the army in the absence of a police force in the Roman empire and would have been another duty drawing soldiers away from the Wall.

▲ The Romano-British settlement at Milking Gap from the air looking south towards the Vallum. The ruins of five round stone houses lie within and beside the farmyard wall, also built of stone

▼ Model of the Romano-British farm at Riding Wood, Northumberland. Three round houses sit within a walled enclosure; the yards would have served as pens for cattle or sheep. The surrounding wall would have helped to keep out wild animals such as wolves and bears

▲ An Iron Age family of the time immediately before the arrival of the Romans in Britain

15

How long was Hadrian's Wall in use?

▲ *The successful reconquest of southern Scotland in the early 140s on the orders of the Emperor Antoninus Pius is recorded on his coinage. This coin was issued in 144 and shows on the reverse the personification of the province, Britannia*

Remarkably, within months of Hadrian's death in July 138, his successor, Antoninus Pius, decided to abandon the newly built Wall and move the frontier forward nearly 100 miles (160 km), building a new Wall across the Forth-Clyde isthmus. This new Wall, the Antonine Wall, was built of turf throughout its length of 40 Roman miles (37 modern miles = 60 km). When completed, it had more forts than Hadrian's Wall, yet it was occupied for only about 20 years. Following another change of emperor, it too was abandoned, this time in favour of a return to Hadrian's Wall.

In the 160s Hadrian's Wall was re-occupied. The Wall and its buildings were repaired and the ditches cleaned out. One new feature was added – a road, the Military Way. Previously the Stanegate, running a mile or so behind the Wall along the river valleys, had been the main line of communication across the isthmus.

Twenty years later there began a troublesome time for the Wall. There was a major invasion of the province by the northern tribes during which a Roman general was killed with his army. A new governor, Ulpius Marcellus, was sent out to deal with the problem, but victory took four years to achieve. The British army then rebelled and even tried to set up its own emperor.

On 31 December 192 the Emperor Commodus was assassinated. The governor of Britain, Clodius Albinus, became one of the contenders for the succession.

Albinus led an army to the Continent but was defeated by Septimius Severus near Lyon in 197. Severus, now ruler of the whole empire, sent a new governor to the island. He found both the principal barbarian tribes in the north, the Caledones and the Maeatae, eager for war. Unable to mount an offensive himself, he had to purchase peace by the payment of a considerable sum of money. Even so, trouble rumbled on in the north for the next ten years.

In 208, Severus came to Britain with his two sons intent on solving the problem of the British frontier for good. His aim was to complete the conquest of the island. He campaigned against the Caledones and Maeatae and forced them to submit, but at the time of his death at York in February 211 both tribes were in revolt. His sons reversed his policy, making treaties with the enemy, evacuating their territory, and returning to Rome.

Throughout the third century little is heard of north Britain. So far as we can tell, the frontier was at peace. But, at the very end of the century, in 297, we first hear of the new enemy which was to menace the northern

▲ *The Emperor Constantius campaigned against the Picts shortly before his death in 306*

▼ *Turret 41a was eliminated in the late second century when the Wall was rebuilt across its site. The original internal north wall of the turret can be seen behind the later wall blocking the recess*

frontier – the Picts. The Emperor Constantius campaigned against them shortly before his death in 306, as probably did his son Constantine the Great a few years later. In the next generation, in 342/3, the situation was so serious that Constantine's son, the Emperor Constans, came over to the island in winter. Trouble in the 360s peaked in a conspiracy of all the barbarian tribes in 367. Order was restored, and the defences repaired, by Count Theodosius. But in 382 the Picts and the Irish again invaded, only to be repulsed by Magnus Maximus, shortly before he crossed to the Continent in an abortive attempt to claim the purple.

Hadrian's Wall slid into obscurity; it did not end in catastrophe. In 407 the British army chose their own emperor, Constantine III, and he also departed for the Continent to try to win the imperial throne. He probably took his field army and other troops with him. Britain became cut off from the rest of the empire; and rule from Rome was never restored.

No mass evacuation of Roman troops and officials took place. British cities – the basis of local government in the island – were left to manage their own affairs. It is doubtful if the army on the Wall was withdrawn in 407. It was no longer a mobile force, merely a static frontier garrison. When the pay chests failed to arrive the soldiers would have turned to other activities, such as farming and brigandage, while others may have left to seek opportunities elsewhere. The Wall was left to decay.

▲ *On the reverse of this medallion, he is shown being greeted by the city of London, after recovering Britain from the usurper Allectus in 296*

◀ *The Picts have left many records on their enigmatic symbol stones. This stone, from Aberlemno and probably dating to the eighth century, shows a group of Picts hunting. The Pictish nation was formed by the amalgamation of the tribes earlier recorded occupying the land north of the Forth, including the Caledones*

▼ *This inscription from Chesters records the provision of a water supply (aqua adducta) by the Second Cohort of Asturians (which had originally been raised in north-west Spain) under the governor Ulpius Marcellus. The early third century saw the improvement of facilities at many forts along the Wall*

▲ *The Antonine Wall was built in the 140s from Bo'ness on the Forth to Old Kilpatrick on the Clyde. Its main surviving feature today is the ditch. This view shows the ditch crossing Croy Hill*

After the Romans left

We know very little of life on Hadrian's Wall during the centuries following its abandonment by Rome. The English (Anglo-Saxons) began to take over in southern and eastern Britain in the fifth and sixth centuries, and, in the north, in the late sixth and the seventh centuries. North of the Wall, it was in the fifth century that the Scots from Ireland began to settle on the west coast of the country which was later named after them, Scotland.

A few Anglo-Saxon objects have been found towards the east end of Hadrian's Wall, but in the main the newcomers largely passed it by. Perhaps some descendants of soldiers continued to live in the forts or civil settlements, we cannot say. Vindolanda is unique in that a post-Roman inscription has been found there: this is the tombstone of a certain Brigomaglos, who died about 500. We do know, however, that the Wall was not totally forgotten, though garbled stories now grew up about it. Gildas, writing about 540, knew of both Hadrian's Wall and the Antonine Wall, but placed their construction 250 years too late and thought they had been built against the Picts and Scots, an erroneous view of the function of Hadrian's Wall that has persisted to the present day. The Venerable Bede in his *History of the English Church and People*, completed in 731,

▲ *Nearly a thousand inscriptions on stone have been found on Hadrian's Wall. These have been carefully recorded and published. This inscription was found in Birdoswald fort in 1821 and first published in the Carlisle Patriot for 16 June 1821. It is now in the undercroft of Lanercost Priory. The altar was dedicated to the holy god Silvanus by the venatores Bannienses, which was probably a regiment based at Birdoswald in the third century. Silvanus was god of the woods*

▲ *John Clayton of Chesters (1792-1890) who did so much to preserve the Wall and reveal its secrets in the nineteenth century*

followed Gildas on the date and function of Hadrian's Wall, but added the information that it was eight feet wide and twelve high. These dimensions may well have resulted from his own observations as his monastery lay close to the eastern end of the Wall.

Through the centuries which followed, the Wall was frequently plundered for stone used to build the churches, houses and field walls of northern England. Stones might be carried many miles: inscriptions from Birdoswald have been found 5 miles (8 km) away at Lanercost Priory, for example. This use of the Wall as a convenient quarry continued into the late nineteenth century. Despoilers occasionally sought other plunder. During the reign of King John, in 1201, there was an excavation to seek treasure, but none was found. In later centuries the local gentry carried off inscriptions and

sculpture to adorn their houses.

The era of serious observation and enquiry began in the sixteenth century and early antiquarian accounts are still useful sources of information about the Wall. It was only in 1840, however, that the whole of the frontier complex was first correctly attributed to Hadrian, though this was not immediately generally accepted. It was about the same time that archaeological excavation began on the Wall. John Clayton of Chesters, during the course of a long life from 1792 to 1890, acquired many miles of the Wall and several of its forts. He disinterred wall, turrets, milecastles and parts of the forts at Chesters and Housesteads: the museum at Chesters, though not built until after his death is essentially his collection of relics.

Modern excavation began in the 1890s and still continues. During the years up to 1939 many of the major problems concerning the Wall were solved through excavation. Nevertheless there still remain large areas where our knowledge is very imperfect, in particular concerning the history and lay-out of forts and the history of the whole Wall through the third and fourth centuries.

It was in 1933 that Corbridge was taken into the care of the nation and this was followed in 1934 by three sections of Hadrian's Wall. Since that date several miles of the Wall, including turrets, milecastles and three forts, have come into state care; they are all now looked after by English Heritage. In addition other parts of the Wall are owned by local authorities, including the forts at South Shields, Wallsend, Rudchester and Birdoswald, while the National Trust owns the fort at Housesteads and the Wall thereabouts. All these fragments of the great frontier complex built over 1850 years ago are carefully preserved in the public interest and open to all visitors.

▶ *Many miles of Hadrian's Wall are in the care of English Heritage. Looking after these sections is a full-time task. Here English Heritage's masons are consolidating a length of Wall. Before work begins the Wall is photographed and drawn; the stones are then numbered and removed in short stretches until good Roman mortar is found; after cleaning and washing, the stones are replaced using modern mortar. No attempt is made to 'restore' the Wall: no new stones are added*

ENGLISH HERITAGE

MUSEUM OF ANTIQUITIES (NEWCASTLE)

▲ *Revd John Hodgson (1779-1845) was the first to suggest that Hadrian's Wall, its forts and the Vallum were all built under Hadrian*

◀ *Many excavations on the line of the Wall are sponsored by English Heritage. Here a team is at work surveying the Wall. Recent work in the central sector suggests that the Wall may have been plastered or whitewashed, and that the original clay or soil bonding the rubble was replaced by mortar at the end of the second century or early in the third century. An extra stone tower has also been found at Peel Gap, midway between turrets 39a and b*

ENGLISH HERITAGE

19

Where to see Hadrian's Wall

Wall: Heddon, Sewingshields–Steel Rigg, Cawfields, Walltown Crags, Gilsland–Birdoswald

Vallum: Sewingshields

Vallum crossing: Benwell

Turrets: 7b (Denton), 26b (Brunton), 29a (Black Carts), 33b, 34a, 35a (Sewingshields–Housesteads), 41a (Shield-on-the-Wall at Cawfields), 44b (Mucklebank), 45a (Walltown), 48a and b (Willowford), 49b, 51a, 51b, 52a (Turf Wall)

Milecastles: 35 (Sewingshields), 37 (Housesteads), 39 (Castle Nick), 42 (Cawfields), 48 (Poltross Burn in Gilsland), 49 (Harrow's Scar)

Forts: South Shields, Wallsend, Newcastle (beside Keep), Chesters, Housesteads, Vindolanda/Chesterholm, Birdoswald

Bath-houses: Chesters, Vindolanda/Chesterholm

Civil settlements: Housesteads, Vindolanda/Chesterholm

Temples: Benwell, Carrawburgh, Corbridge

Bridges: Chesters, Willowford

Supply base: South Shields

Military base: Corbridge

Stanegate forts: Corbridge, Vindolanda/Chesterholm

Pre-Wall towers: Walltown (45a), Pike Hill

Museums

There are site museums at Chesters, Corbridge, Housesteads, South Shields and Vindolanda. The other two principal museums for the Wall are:

Carlisle Museum, Castle Street, Carlisle.
Museum of Antiquities, The Quadrangle, Newcastle upon Tyne. Both contain many objects and inscriptions found on and near to Hadrian's Wall, as well as models.

The Roman Army Museum at Carvoran is devoted to reconstructions of Hadrian's Wall and the soldiers who manned it.

IMAGES This page: *Hadrian's Wall at Cawfields sits on top of precipitous crags*

SOUTH SHIELDS ROMAN FORT

The very end of the frontier complex lay at South Shields where a fort sat on the low hill overlooking the mouth of the river Tyne. The archaeological ruins here are in the care of Tyne and Wear Museums.

The visible fort at South Shields was probably built under Marcus Aurelius (161-80), replacing an earlier fort dating to the reign of Hadrian. Most of the visible buildings are of local sandstone but in the earliest stages of building magnesian limestone was used, for example in the double granary. The water settling tanks show that the fort was supplied by an aqueduct. The original west gate was reconstructed to full size in 1986-7.

In the early third century the south wall of the fort was taken down and the fort extended, increasing its area from 3.9 to 5.1 acres (1.6-2.1 ha). Many of the buildings were replaced by 22 granaries. These changes, converting the fort into a supply-base, were probably connected with Septimius Severus' campaigns and projected occupation of Scotland. After 211, when the Scottish campaigns ended, its purpose had to change: presumably its use now was to store supplies for the units of the northern frontier. Several of the granaries and the headquarters building of the supply base are visible.

After the buildings of the supply-base had been destroyed by fire in the late third or early fourth century, the interior of the fort was completely replanned. Twelve barracks were built in the southern part of the fort, ten of them re-using the walls of granaries. A new headquarters building was built on the site of the original headquarters and a large courtyard house, with a dining room and hypocausts, occupied the south-east corner of the fort. This building maybe associated with the replacement of cohors V Gallorum by a new unit, the numerus barbicorum Tigrisiensium, a unit of bargemen from the river Tigris. Activity in the fort continued into the fifth century and perhaps beyond.

▲ A replica of the west gate, rebuilt in 1986 on the original foundations, now serves as a museum. Detailed research has resulted in the most authentic reconstruction of a fort gate anywhere in the Roman Empire

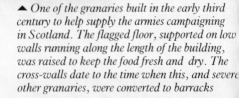

▲ Mars, the god of war, on a sword found at South Shields

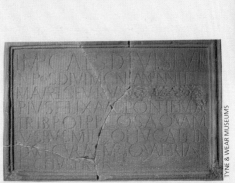

◄ This inscription records the installation of a water supply for cohors V Gallorum in 222 during the reign of the Emperor Severus Alexander

▲ One of the granaries built in the early third century to help supply the armies campaigning in Scotland. The flagged floor, supported on low walls running along the length of the building, was raised to keep the food fresh and dry. The cross-walls date to the time when this, and severe other granaries, were converted to barracks

TYNE & WEAR MUSEUMS

ENGLISH HERITAGE

◀ *Tombstone of Victor the Moor, freedman of Numerianus a cavalryman in the First Cavalry Regiment of Asturians, who died at the age of 20. Many Roman soldiers appear to have kept slaves*

TYNE & WEAR MUSEUMS

ENGLISH HERITAGE

▲ *Most forts contained a strong room where the unit's and the soldiers' money was kept. The lower stones were held together by cramps*

ENGLISH HERITAGE

▲ *The plain tombstone of Barathes of Palmyra found at Corbridge and the highly decorated tombstone of Regina, wife of Barathes of Palmyra, from South Shields: the two inscriptions probably refer to the same man. The story told on the tombstone reflects the cosmopolitan nature of the Roman world. Barathes came from Syria; he was perhaps a flag bearer rather than a dealer in flags. While in Britain he bought a slave girl Regina, of the tribe of the Catuvellauni; he freed her and married her. Regina's elaborate tombstone is carved in Palmyrene style and suggests that a stone-carver from that city worked in South Shields*

◀ *The communal latrine was provided for the use of all the soldiers in the regiment. The soldiers cleaned themselves with moss or sponges*   23

Tour of South Shields

The **entrance** lies through the reconstructed **west gate**, which houses a series of displays. The lay-out of the fort can best be understood by viewing it from the top of the gate, after which the visitor should proceed to the **north gate** by way of the **north-west angle tower**.

The headquarters building dates from the late third or early fourth century. The rear rooms of this building include a strong room (with part of a window sill surviving); the offices on either side contain hypocausts. Behind is the well which lay in the courtyard of the second-century headquarters.

Parts of eight **granaries** are visible in the central area: two preserve the partitions of later barracks. South of the granaries the **headquarters building** associated with the supply base can be seen. The junction of the original east **fort wall** and its extension is marked by the remains of the south-east angle tower. Continue past the third century **communal latrine** to the later **south-east angle**, where the chamfered base of the fort wall is preserved. Beside, is a large **courtyard house**, probably built for the commanding officer. Walk on past the **south gate** and **south-west angle tower** to the site **museum and archaeology centre** where recent finds from the excavations are displayed.

▲ *South Shields fort from the air looking west*

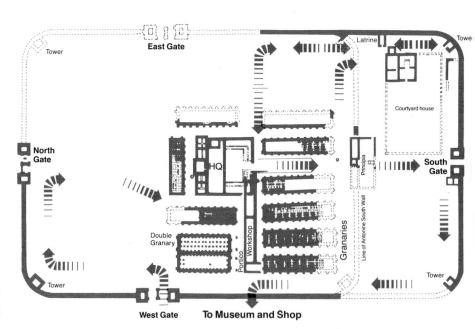

24

WALLSEND ROMAN FORT

The fort at Wallsend lies at the eastern end of the Wall. It was built under Hadrian and excavations have shown that it was occupied to the end of Roman Britain. Much of its plan has also been revealed by excavation, but today little Roman stonework is visible. The headquarters building has been consolidated and the line of the fort walls and gates marked out by North Tyneside District Council. Tyne and Wear Museums maintain the Wallsend Heritage Centre, where some of the finds from the fort are displayed, visible by arrangement.

▲ Bronze portable shrine, probably to the god Mercury and dating to the fourth century, found in the fort at Wallsend

▲ Bronze figurine of the goddess Fortuna, found at Wallsend

◄ To the west of the fort a full-sized replica of Hadrian's Wall has been built immediately behind the original foundations

▼ Wallsend from the air looking south. The outline of the fort and, in the foreground, the barrack-blocks have been marked out. In the centre of the fort lies the headquarters building. A short section of wall ran down to the river from the far corner of the fort

NEWCASTLE TO HEDDON-ON-THE-WALL

The Military Road, constructed in the aftermath of the 1745 Jacobite Uprising led by Bonnie Prince Charlie, carries the modern visitor westwards from Newcastle. Beside the road are scattered fragments of the Wall. These were all built to the original specification for the Wall, 10 Roman feet thick, often referred to as 'broad wall'.

The fort at Benwell is buried beneath 1930s housing, but two important fragments can be seen. South of the fort the causeway leading across the Vallum ditch is preserved, while a short distance away, but in a different housing estate, is the temple of a local god, Antenociticus.

A mile to the west, immediately beside the modern road, is Denton Hall turret (7b). Built of unusually large stones, it still retains the platform in the corner which probably served as the base for a ladder leading to the upper floors.

At Heddon-on-the-Wall can be seen the longest visible stretch of broad wall, 10 Roman feet thick. The stones here were originally set in puddled clay, but this has now been replaced by mortar for stability. A circular structure in the thickness of the wall is a kiln of post-Roman date.

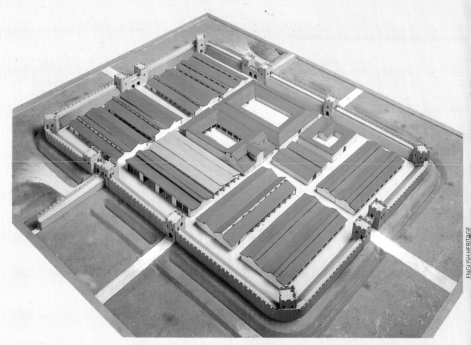

▲ A model of the Roman fort at Benwell as it might have appeared. The fort sits astride the Wall

▼ A model of the Vallum crossing with the gate closed to traffic. The gate was controlled from the fort side showing that the Vallum faced south

▼ The Vallum crossing at Benwell looking north-east. The road leading south from the fort passes through the gate. Heavy wear led to repeated resurfacing of the road and this is represented by the steps in its surface. The masonry of the surviving gate pier is amongst the best anywhere on the Wall. The ditch is now only half its original depth

◄ *Denton Hall turret (7b) looking west. The turret is recessed into the thickness of the Wall. To the left is a platform which may have formed the base for a ladder leading to the first floor and above*

◄ *The broad wall and ditch at Heddon-on-the-Wall looking east. The rubble core of the Wall was usually clay-bonded with only the facing stones mortared. Traces of mortar still adhering to the faces of some stones suggest that the Wall may have looked more white than brown when built*

▲ *The head of Antenociticus formerly graced a statue which probably stood in the apse.*

◄ *The temple of Antenociticus at Benwell with its two altars to the god. The altars are copies: the originals are in the Museum of Antiquities, Newcastle*

CHESTERS ROMAN FORT

Chesters fort lies in the pleasant valley of the river North Tyne. Here, in the parkland laid out by the Clayton family in the early nineteenth century, can be viewed remains of the fort, the well-preserved bath-house and the remarkable museum built 80 years ago to house the great collection brought together by John Clayton of Chesters.

An inscription found as recently as 1978 demonstrates that Chesters was built for *ala Augusta ob virtutem appellata*, a cavalry regiment 'called Augusta for valour'. Other units are attested at the fort in the second century, but from the end of the century Chesters was the base for the Second Cavalry Regiment of Asturians (originally raised in Spain), which remained here for 200 years.

Chesters was built astride the Wall with three of its four main gates opening north of the Wall. Access south of the Wall was increased by the provision of an extra pair of side gates. The circuit of defences, only part of which can be seen, was strengthened by the provision of towers at the four corners of the fort and at intervals along the walls. Two ditches, now silted up, lay beyond the fort wall. Outside the fort was the bath-house, one of the best preserved buildings of Roman Britain, and a civil settlement, which has not been excavated.

▶ *A reconstruction illustration by Alan Sorrell of the fort and civil settlement at Chesters*

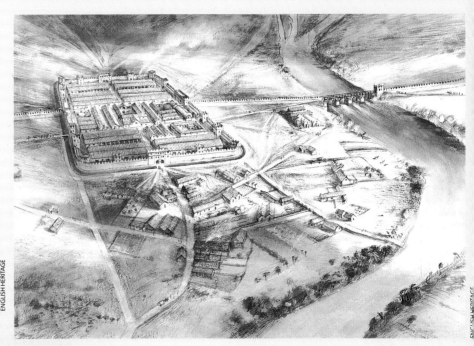

▲ *Statue of a river god, possibly Neptune, found in the commanding officer's bath-house*

◀ *The commanding officer's bath-house, showing the furnace and the raised floor of the hot room behind*

▶ *The fort bath-house, looking across the changing room to the steam range. The niches to the right may have been for clothes or small statues: the arches were probably originally window heads. The latrine lies to the left*

◄ *The strong room. Here the regiment's money was kept. Access was from the adjacent shrine in the foreground, where a guard was on duty at all times*

▶ *Statue of the goddess Juno Dolichena standing on a heifer*

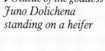

▲ *The headquarters building. In the foreground is the courtyard and beyond it the assembly hall and the back rooms*

▲ *A reconstruction by Alan Sorrell of the assembly hall with the tribunal to the right, and the back rooms in the headquarters building*

▲ *This glass flask, found at Corbridge, carried the oil used in bath-houses. Oil was used instead of soap*

▼ *A reconstruction of the regimental bath-house by Alan Sorrell*

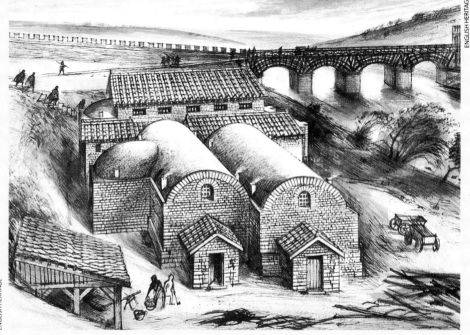

Tour of Chesters

On leaving the custodian's office turn left along the path to the fort. Ahead lies the **north gate**. Two roadways passed through this gate. An aqueduct entered the fort below the west (right) road. Turn right along the path leading to the **west gate**. Here the iron collars which formerly held the door pivots can be seen. A water channel leads into the north (right) guard chamber, and beyond it is an oven. Hadrian's Wall abuts the south (left) guard chamber. Continue on round the perimeter of the fort past an interval tower to the **south gate**. This shows much evidence of use; the road was finally raised 30 in (800 mm) above the Hadrianic level. Another interval tower lies beyond the gate. Turn left at the angle tower and walk to the **minor east gate**, noting, to the left, the columns of a barrack-block verandah. Leave the fort here and turn right down to the **bath-house**.

The **bath-house** is a complex building, rendered more difficult to understand by the lack of floors in the heated rooms. Pass through the **porch** into the **changing room**: the function of the seven niches is uncertain. To the left is the **latrine**, ahead the door leading into the heated rooms. To the right of the first room, a vestibule, are the two rooms of the **hot dry suite** (some of the flags are modern): note the stone door jambs (wood would have warped) and the furnace outside the room. To the left of the vestibule lay the **cold room** containing a basin for cold water and, ahead, a cold bath later replaced by the smaller cold bath to the left. A cold bath was necessary to close the pores before leaving the bath-house. Beyond the vestibule is the **steam range**. The floors have been removed so today we walk around in the basement. The first room, formerly two, was the hottest and therefore the last in the sequence: the two warm rooms to the left were entered first by the bather. At the far end of the hot room lies the furnace, where the boiler formerly sat (at one time this may have served as a hot bath). To the right is the hot bath with a window above: note the plaster on the wall beside the bath. Before leaving walk round the back of the bath-house to see the voussoirs (wedge-shaped stones) from the barrel-vaulted ceiling: these are made from a lightweight rock called tufa.

Beyond the fort are slight remains of the west abutment of the bridge (see page 32). Return to the fort and enter the **east gate**. This is one of the most impressive gates on Hadrian's Wall, one pier still standing to the beginning of the arch. Pass through the gate, go round to the right and step over the wall into the centurion's suite of the **barrack-block**. Walk through this and along the road between the two barrack-

30

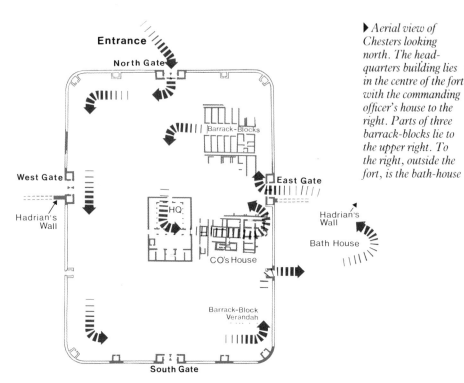

Aerial view of Chesters looking north. The headquarters building lies in the centre of the fort with the commanding officer's house to the right. Parts of three barrack-blocks lie to the upper right. To the right, outside the fort, is the bath-house

▲ *Reconstruction by Peter Connolly of a pair of facing barrack-blocks at Chesters fort*

◀ *The barrack-blocks today. The drain would have been covered by stone slabs*

NORTHUMBRIA AIRFOTOS

blocks: the individual rooms, each thought to have been occupied by eight soldiers, were probably divided into two by timber partitions.

Outside the modern gate to this enclosure turn left and, bearing right, cross the field to enter the **headquarters building**. The large courtyard is surrounded by a colonnade: possibly notices were pinned up here. Beside the well, on the paving, is a phallic symbol, a good-luck charm. Continue into the assembly hall, with its dais or tribunal to the right, now reduced to its lowest courses. Beyond, the back rooms are well preserved. The two to the right were probably used by the clerks of the regimental office, and the two to the left by the accounts clerks. In the centre was the unit's shrine where a statue of the emperor and the regiment's standards would have been placed. Leading off this is the strong room; its oak door disintegrated on excavation.

Leave the headquarters building by the side entrance and examine the **commanding officer's house**. The present maze of rooms is the result of additions and rebuildings over many years: a small bath-house lies at the far end.

Return from here to the **museum**. This was opened in 1903 and has been little altered since that date. It contains many finds from Chesters and other forts on Hadrian's Wall once owned by the Clayton family.

THE CHESTERS AREA

Across the river from Chesters fort lies the east abutment of the bridge over the river North Tyne. A pier embedded in this abutment probably formed part of the Hadrianic bridge. This is thought to have had ten stone piers supporting a timber superstructure carrying a walk across the river. The position of the robbed east abutment of the bridge and a section of the paved riverbed can be seen in the bottom of the later tower.

The visible abutment lay on the east side of the second bridge, which was built in the early third century. A gate tower, the basement of which survives, probably gave access to a bridge consisting of three stone arches. Many carved stones from the superstructure of this bridge remain on the site. In the later Roman period a water channel, probably serving a mill south of the bridge, was led through the tower basement.

Eastwards from Chesters Bridge and a few yards from the modern road lies Brunton turret (26b). This still stands nearly 8½ ft

(2.4 m) high. From its western side runs the Wall built to the original specification, 10 Roman feet thick. On the east side a much narrower Wall, about 6 ft thick, rides up over the turret's wing wall. The differences probably result from changes in plan during construction of the Wall.

Half a mile to the east of Brunton turret a short length of Wall lies at Planetrees. Here there is another point where the Wall was reduced from the original 10 Roman feet, in this case to about 6½ ft. It is clear that the soldiers laying the Wall's foundations had progressed quicker than the builders of the superstructure as the foundations continue on past the point of reduction. Interestingly the foundation builders also appear to have laid the drain, most of which is incorporated into the narrow wall. West of Chesters a mile length of Wall climbing up to Limestone Corner contains a turret at Black Carts (29a). This turret seems to have continued in occupation into the fourth century.

▲ *Brunton turret (26b)*

▼ *Chesters bridge abutment. The earlier pier can be discerned to the left, within the masonry of the abutment of the later bridge. The tower* *probably provided access to this later bridge. To the right of the tower are the massive cover slabs of the late Roman water-channel*

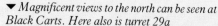

▲ *Here, at Planetrees, the Wall was reduced in thickness from 10 to 6½ Roman feet. This would have reduced the work-load of the legionaries and may have been ordered to that end*

▼ *Magnificent views to the north can be seen at Black Carts. Here also is turret 29a*

CARRAWBURGH: TEMPLE TO MITHRAS

The fort is in private ownership, but English Heritage look after an area around it which includes the remarkable temple to the god Mithras. The fort was an addition to the Wall, probably being built in the 130s. By this time, the Vallum had been constructed and its ditch had to be filled, and its mounds levelled, when the fort was built over it. In the third and fourth centuries Carrawburgh was the home of the First Cohort of Batavians, a regiment originally raised from a tribe living at the mouth of the Rhine. The mithraeum (temple to Mithras) was probably constructed by soldiers based in the fort; the three altars found here (copies stand in the temple) were all dedicated by commanding officers of the unit. Mithras was an Eastern god. According to legend he had captured and killed in a cave the primaeval bull, the first creature created on earth and from this slaying sprang the benefits of mankind. So mithraea were dark and gloomy, purposefully resembling caves. Mithras was supported by his attendants, Cautes and Cautopotes.

Mithraism was especially disliked by Christians who saw in the mithraic ritual of taking bread and water a caricature of their own holy sacrament. Thus it may have been Christians rather than barbarians who destroyed this temple in the fourth century, smashing the reredos, the scene depicting Mithras killing the bull, but leaving intact the altars dedicated by commanding officers.

ENGLISH HERITAGE

▲ *This representation of a dog (perhaps an Aberdeen terrier often called a Scottie dog) was probably found in Coventina's Well; like the other contents of the shrine it would have been a gift to the goddess*

North of the mithraeum is Coventina's Well (not in the care of English Heritage). A pool on the site of the sacred spring is all that survives of this temple of the water goddess Coventina. 13,490 coins were found here when the temple was examined in 1876, as well as inscriptions, sculptures, pottery vessels, incense burners and brooches, all thrown in to honour, or to help win favours from, the goddess. Many of these objects can be seen at Chesters Museum.

MUSEUM OF ANTIQUITIES (NEWCASTLE)

TOUR

From the carpark follow the path round the side of the fort.

In front of the mithraeum one slab of the water-tank of the shrine of the Nymphs sticks out of the turf. Inside the door of the mithraeum is an ante-chapel. This would have been used for the initiation tests which worshippers had to pass before being allowed to proceed to the next grade in the temple hierarchy (there were seven grades: Raven, Bridegroom, Soldier, Lion, Persian, Courier of the Sun and Father). In the right hand corner is a small statue of a mother

ENGLISH HERITAGE

▲ *The mithraeum at Carrawburgh had been buried under peat for over 1600 years before its re-discovery in 1949*

▲ *This full-scale reconstruction of the Carrawburgh mithraeum is in the Museum of Antiquities, Newcastle upon Tyne. It reminds us that Roman buildings and sculptures, now so drab, were once brightly painted. Cautes and Cautopates flank the nave, while above the altars is the tauroctony, the scene of Mithras killing the bull*

goddess – this is a copy, like the other statues and the altars and also the timber posts and wattles. To the left is a hearth, used for ordeals or preparing ritual feasts.

Cautes and Cautopates guard the nave. Here benches lie on either side of a central passage. Worshippers would have reclined on these benches during ceremonies.

At the far end of the temple is the sanctuary containing the altars. On one altar Mithras appears as the Charioteer of the Sun: this stone has been hollowed out behind so that a lamp placed in the receptacle will cause the rays to light up. Above the altars, resting on the projecting stone, would have been a sculpture of Mithras killing the bull. The original altars and sculptures are in the Museum of Antiquities, Newcastle.

HOUSESTEADS ROMAN FORT

▲ *This sculpture of Victory once adorned the east gate*

◄ *Housesteads looking north. The character- istic playing card shape of the fort is clear. Within lay 18 buildings. Visible now are the headquarters building in the centre, the granaries beyond the commanding officer's house to this side, and the hospital to the left. Top right are two barrack-blocks and a storehouse. Outside the fort part of the civil settlement is visible. When built, the fort was surrounded by two ditches, now filled in*

ENGLISH HERITAGE

Housesteads is the best-known fort on Had- rian's Wall. This is as it should be for the fort, perched high on its ridge overlooking the open Northumbrian countryside, conveys the spirit of the past as well as the beauty of the present.

The fort at Housesteads was an addition to Hadrian's Wall, forming part of the second scheme for the frontier. When it was built a turret, erected a short time before on the site, was demolished. In order to gain as much room as possible on the ridge the north wall of the fort was pushed to the very edge of the escarpment. This entailed building deep foundations for the fort wall, and these can still be seen below the threshold of the north gate, though they would once have been covered by a ramp.

Housesteads fort covers 5 acres (2 hec- tares) and was occupied through the third and

fourth centuries by the First Cohort of Tungrians, a unit which had originally been raised from one of the tribes of present-day Belgium. This was an infantry regiment nominally 1000 strong, though in practice it probably only contained 800. The fort was probably built for a similar sized unit. In the third century the Cohort of Tungrians was strengthened by two other units, Notfried's Regiment from Germany, and a unit of Frisians raised from the tribe which lived at the mouth of the river Rhine. Today the buildings exposed are of different periods, reflecting the long and complex history of the site, although the overall layout changed little over the nearly three centuries of occupation.

The fort at Housesteads lay at the centre of a thriving community. All that can now be seen of this civil settlement is the

small group of buildings which are on view outside the south gate of the fort. These buildings probably included shops, inns and, furthest from the fort, a house where, it appears, a murder had been committed and the bodies buried beneath the floor.

On the hillside below the civil settle- ment are a series of terraces. These were originally long, thin fields but it is uncertain whether they are Roman or later in date. Certain other features at Housesteads reflect later occupation. The additions to the south gate and the corn drying kilns here and in the granaries were all in use at the time House- steads was the base for moss troopers – brigands – in the seventeenth century. More recently farming has left its traces, for example in the round enclosure before the museum – this surrounds a well.

Tour

Go first to the **museum**. Here is a display of finds from the site and a model of the fort and civil settlement. On leaving the museum head for the **south gate** ahead. Before entering the fort examine the houses of the **civil settlement** in front of the gate. Notice how the front walls of these buildings line up with the centre of the gate, not the far side, demonstrating that the far (east) portal of the gate had been blocked by the time the houses were built in the third century.

Pass through the gate, noting the wear on the threshold. The eastern guard chamber was extended and the kiln inserted when moss troopers lived here in the seventeenth century. Turn right and continue along the inside of the south wall to the **latrine**. Wooden seats would have covered the main sewer channel, which was fed with water from the adjacent tanks. The small channel was used for washing the sponges used instead of toilet paper.

Proceed on round the fort to the **east gate**, the front gate of the fort. The southern passage of the gate was completely blocked up at some stage in its history and the guard chamber turned into a coal store. The deeply worn wheel-ruts are about 4 ft 8 in (1.4 m) apart. This is the normal width of cart axles from antiquity to the present day, and is reflected by the standard railway gauge of 4 ft 8½ in. Continue on a little way and turn left to pass between the two fourth-century **barrack-blocks**, each built as a series of separate buildings. At the far end, to the right, lies the **north gate**, and beyond it the **turret** demolished when the fort was built; this is now partly obscured by the walls of later buildings.

At the turret turn left to the **granaries**. The first is the best preserved and details of its door (bolted on the inside), stone supports for the floor, and ventilator holes in the walls, can be examined. Walk on to the corner of the second granary. Ahead lie two buildings, the **hospital** to the right (this consists of wards and a large room to the north interpreted as an operating theatre, all ranged round a courtyard) and the **headquarters building** to the left. Immediately before you are the rooms where the regimental clerks worked and where the standards of the unit were housed (the far two rooms have been modified by the insertion of a staircase at the rear). Enter the building by the steps to your left and note the commanding officer's dais on your right facing down the assembly hall. Pass, left, through the courtyard and turn right down the main street of the fort to the **commanding officer's house**, again a series of rooms round an open courtyard. To the right lies the kitchen containing an oven; the

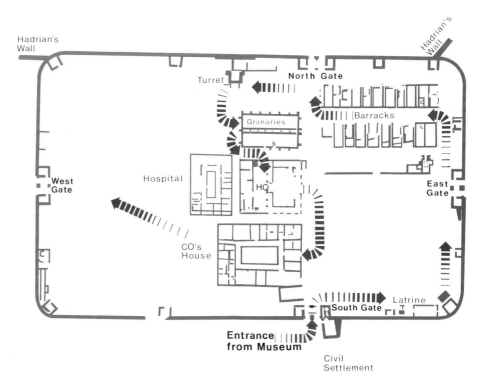

dining room presumably lay hereabouts. The heated room in the centre of the north range served as a bath-suite for a time. A latrine, and its later replacement, lay in the centre of the west range. The basements beside the entrance served as stables.

After viewing the buildings in the central range of the fort walk to the **west (back) gate** of the fort. This preserves two interesting features: the holes for the bar

▲ *This reconstruction shows Housesteads as it might have looked in the third century when the civil settlement had spread over the slopes south of the fort*

which was slotted into place when the gate was closed and, by the front corners of the gate, the marking out lines scored by the masons who built it.

ENGLISH HERITAGE

▲ *This sculpture of Mars was formerly placed over the entrance to the headquarters building. Originally, it will have been brightly painted*

A reconstruction ▲ *of the commanding officer's house by Peter Connolly*

▶ *The commanding officer's house consisted of a range of rooms round an open courtyard. It was a large house, as befitted the commander's status, and provided accommodation for himself, his family and his slaves. In the foreground lies the kitchen containing ovens*

DAVID J BREEZE

◀ *The headquarters building looking south-west. The assembly hall in the centre is flanked, left, by the courtyard, and, right, by the rooms for the administrative staff*

▶ *The west gate. Towers flank the two roads passing through the gate*

◀ *The communal latrine in the south-east corner of the fort. A complex arrangement of tanks and channels ensured the supply of water to this building, and a main drain carried the sewage out of the fort. The wooden seats over the sewer channel have long since rotted, but the joist holes remain. The entrance was originally at the far end, where a blocked doorway is still visible. The latrine and the hospital emphasise the Roman army's care for hygiene and health. Throughout history, disease has killed more soldiers than fighting*

▼ *The tombstone of Anicius Ingenuus, a doctor (medicus) in the First Cohort of Tungrians, who died at Housesteads aged only 25. The hospital at Housesteads lies behind the headquarters building. The reason for the carving of the hare on top of the tombstone is not known*

▼ *A reconstruction of the granaries by Peter Connolly. The soldier carries a sack, which we know were used in Roman times. The grain may have been stored inside the granary in bins or in sacks*

▼ *Food of all kinds was stored in the granaries on a raised floor supported on stone pillars. Ventilating slots in the wall helped air to circulate below the floor and keep it fresh. The two granaries were probably originally one large building with a colonnade down the centre*

HOUSESTEADS TO SEWINGSHIELDS

Two miles of Hadrian's Wall between Housesteads and Sewingshields are in the care of English Heritage and another mile is owned by the National Trust. This sector is best reached from Housesteads. Although perhaps less spectacular than the crags to the west, it contains many interesting features and there are magnificent views north, south and westwards to Housesteads, Cuddy's Crags and beyond.

Below the north-east corner of Housesteads fort is the Knag Burn gate, which was probably inserted into the Wall in the fourth century. For the next mile no Wall is visible but between turret 35a and milecastle 35 several short lengths have been exposed. One stretch is particularly interesting for, in a dip, the Wall is stepped down on one side while riding with the contours on the other. In places the foundations are as wide as 11 Roman feet, though the Wall itself, built after the decision to narrow the Wall, is usually about 8 feet.

Milecastle 35 was excavated between 1978 and 1980. There is now no north gate to this milecastle but the rebuilt north wall has destroyed any evidence which may have existed for a gate in the Hadrianic period. The original barrack accommodation in the south-east corner of the milecastle is overlain by its early third-century successor. The jumble of walls in the western half of the milecastle belong to third and fourth century buildings. The site was re-occupied in the Middle Ages when a farm was built here.

Turret 34a lies beyond Sewingshields farm. It has unusually short wing walls. Another feature shared with the other two turrets visible in this stretch is that it was abandoned in the later second century.

No ditch was dug along the front of the crags – except in the dips – but a little beyond turret 34a, as the Wall descends from the crags, the ditch suddenly starts on the left. Almost at the end of this stretch is turret 33b. A few yards further on, the Vallum sweeps in from the right. Eastwards from here the Wall and the Vallum run close together as they head for Newcastle.

▲ Turret 34a has very short wing walls. Part of the wall blocking the internal recess has been removed to reveal the original north wall of the turret. Beside the blocking wall is a platform. Possibly this was where the soldiers slept

▲ Turret 33b looking east. This turret went out of use in the later second century. At first the door was blocked up and then the turret was demolished down to the bottom four courses and the recess on the north side blocked up, perhaps to eliminate the resulting weak point in the Wall, or to allow a walk along the top of the Wall to be carried across the site of the turret

◀ An aerial view of milecastle 35 and the Wall from the north-east. The recently excavated milecastle is perched on the very edge of the crag: a north gate was clearly superfluous here

◀ The Vallum at Sewingshields. The modern road drops dramatically into the Vallum ditch. Set back on either side of the ditch is a mound: on the south lip an extra mound is probably the result of later cleaning out of the ditch

HOUSESTEADS TO STEEL RIGG

The three-mile stretch of Hadrian's Wall from the fort at Housesteads over Cuddy's Crags, Hotbank Crags and Peel Crags to Steel Rigg is the most spectacular section of the whole Wall. It is owned by the National Trust. There is a splendid, strenuous walk along the Wall between Housesteads and Steel Rigg car park. This can be started at either end, but for convenience it is described from east (Housesteads) to west.

A short walk of less than half a mile along the top of the Wall leads to milecastle 37. This is one of the best-preserved milecastles on the Wall. Part of an inscription found here demonstrates that it was built by the Second Legion. The gates were built of the large stones which are the hallmark of this legion's work at milecastles. The north gate here is particularly well-preserved. The east half of the milecastle is occupied by a stone-built barrack-block: the back walls of the building have been destroyed. This barrack is large enough to have housed eight men. Those visitors not wishing to continue to Steel Rigg can return to the fort along the path which follows the Military Way south of the Wall.

The Wall strides on from Housesteads milecastle over Cuddy's Crags. John Clayton of Chesters was responsible for the clearing of this stretch of Wall from its accumulated debris in the nineteenth century.

Along the south face can be seen many junctions where presumably different building gangs met. Other aspects of construction are interesting. On a gentle slope, for example, the courses follow the contours. When the slope steepens the courses are laid horizontally and the Wall stepped down the hill. No ditch is necessary along most of this sector, but it re-appears on the low ground at Hotbank and again at Steel Rigg.

One Roman mile west of Housesteads milecastle lie the hollows which marked the robbed-out walls of Hotbank milecastle. Two inscriptions of the Second Legion have been found here, one fallen from the north gate, the other from the south. It can be seen that there is no break in the ditch in front of the north gate. A few yards walk south along the track leads to the ruins of the native farmstead of Milking Gap (to the right of the track).

The Wall runs on along the crags overlooking Crag Lough. A particularly fine stretch by Highshields Crags survives to a height of 10 feet. The next milecastle sits in Castle Nick. This is not the same type of milecastle as those at Housesteads (37) and Hotbank (38); in fact it is the only milecastle of this particular type to be seen on Hadrian's Wall and was probably built by the Sixth Legion. The gates are not as originally constructed, having been later modified.

The last stretch of the Wall before the car park at Steel Rigg runs along Peel Crags. Here lies an extra tower, only discovered in 1987. Beyond the car park is the highest point on the Wall at Winshields Crags. The earthworks of the unexcavated milecastle 40 may be viewed here. Part of this length of the Wall is owned by the National Trust; the rest is in the care of English Heritage.

▶ *Aerial view of Hadrian's Wall looking east from Hotbank Crags*

ENGLISH HERITAGE

▲ *Milecastle 37 (Housesteads). Several of the arch stones survive at the north gate. The gate was narrowed at an unknown date*

DAVID SHERLOCK

▲ *Milecastle 39 (Castle Nick) looking north-west. Occupation of this milecastle continued into the late fourth century*

NORTHUMBRIA AIRFOTOS

VINDOLANDA/CHESTERHOLM

The extensive remains at Vindolanda/Chesterholm – fort, civil settlement, reconstructions and museum – are owned by the Vindolanda Trust. The visible fort and the nearby milestone are in the care of English Heritage.

There were several forts at Vindolanda/Chesterholm before Hadrian's Wall was built. These are not visible, being buried deep below the later fort and its civil settlement. When Hadrian's Wall was built a new fort appears to have been constructed at Vindolanda/Chesterholm. Later in the second century this was rebuilt and troops continued to be based here into the early fifth century. The garrison during the third and fourth centuries was the Fourth Cohort of Gauls, a mixed infantry and cavalry regiment originally raised in what is now France.

The civil settlement is the most extensive such site to be seen on Hadrian's Wall, and indeed anywhere in Britain. Here are exposed the lower courses of houses and shops, a building thought to be an official rest-house for the imperial post (*mansio*) and the regiment's bath-house. There are also two burial tombs visible beside the reconstructions. The civil settlement was first built in the middle of the second century and it continued in occupation, with a short break, until the late third century. Most of the buildings of the very last phase of occupation towards the end of the fourth century have been removed to reveal the earlier buildings.

▲ *The headquarters building with, in the foreground, one of the heated rooms added to the corner back room*

▼ *The regimental clerks worked in this room at the back of the headquarters building. The front panel would have been balanced by a second on the other side of the entrance. A panel lying in the central room bears traces of wear on the top and contains sockets for metal bars*

Finds at Vindolanda

▲ *This betrothal medallion is a rare find in Britain. Made of Whitby jet, it was probably carved in York*

▲ *Many leather shoes have been found in the civil settlement. This is a lady's slipper, stamped with the maker's name, L. AEB. THALES T.F.: Lucius Aebutius Thales, son of Titus*

▲ *This fragment of a letter on a wooden writing-tablet records the sending of socks, sandals and underpants, probably to a soldier stationed at Vindolanda. Both sides of the document (shown here) were written on, in pen and ink*

▲ *A cloth fragment from the pre-Hadrianic fort*

Tour

Visitors will probably approach the site along the Stanegate, arriving at the western car park. A joint admission ticket is available. A visit to the **reconstructions**, passing the **wells** on the right, is recommended first. Here are a section of stone wall with turret and ditch, a length of turf wall and ditch and a timber milecastle gate.

▲ *A full-scale reconstruction of a turret and length of Wall at Vindolanda/Chesterholm*

Return, past the **burial tombs**, to the main path and the **civil settlement**. The buildings here were first constructed in the mid-second century. Visit the **mansio** with its rooms, kitchen, bath-house (back left) and latrine, round an open courtyard. Across the road lies a large **house** with three rooms on either side of a corridor. This was later divided into two houses. Behind this lies the unit's **bath-house**, which still retains some of its original wall-plaster. Return to the main path and walk along the road to the fort. The houses here approach close to the fort wall, being built, in the third century, over the filled-in fort ditches.

Enter the **fort** at the **west gate**, which has only one passage-way flanked by towers. Cross to the **headquarters building**. This follows the normal design, except that the front verandah and the courtyard aisles served as storehouses, while small rooms were added to the rear of the back-rooms. There is no strongroom, but a pit was provided to house the money chests. Several walls broke their backs over the remains of an earlier headquarters building, visible in places.

Leave the headquarters building by the front entrance and continue on to the **north gate**. To the right lie some round structures, possibly houses, destroyed by the construction of the fort wall, and, in the north-east corner of the fort, the **latrine**. Walk on along the east wall, out of the **east gate** (which unusually has no flanking towers), and down to the **museum**, noting the well-preserved fort wall to right and left of the gate.

▲ *Vindolanda/ Chesterholm from the air looking east. The fort lies in the centre. The civil settlement straddles the road leading out of the near (west) gate; the bath-house lies to the left of the road. The reconstructions can be seen to the right*

▼ *This Roman milestone on the Stanegate still stands where it was originally erected*

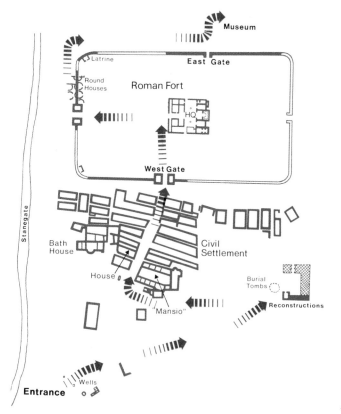

41

CAWFIELDS TO WALLTOWN

The milecastle at Cawfields sits awkwardly on the hillside, cut off to the west by the raw edge of a modern quarry. It was excavated nearly 150 years ago by John Clayton of Chesters. Today it is hard to imagine how the internal buildings could have been arranged sensibly within it, and no trace of any has survived. The massive masonry of the gates has yielded an inscription recording that the milecastle was built by the Second Legion.

A dramatic stretch of Wall runs eastwards from the milecastle for two-thirds of a Roman mile past Thorny Doors. Here is one of the highest standing sections of Hadrian's Wall. A little further on is turret 41a, demolished in the late second century.

Three miles west of Cawfields the Wall snakes over Walltown Crags. Here again the modern topography has been altered by quarrying, thus chopping the Wall into short stretches. On the steep slope of Mucklebank Crag lies turret 44b, its view obscured to the east by the hill on which it sits, but with an impressive vista to the west. A little further on is turret 45a, originally built as a free-standing tower. At the west end of Walltown Crags, beside the fort at Carvoran, is the Roman Army Museum.

▲ *Turret 44b on Mucklebank Crags is unusual in that it sits in an angle of the Wall*

◄ *Cawfields Milecastle (42) hanging on the hillside on this dramatic stretch*

▲ *A most impressive stretch of Wall climbs over Walltown Crags*

▲ *Turret 45a was built as a free-standing tower before the Wall. It probably served as a look-out post in advance of the forts on the Stanegate*

◄ *The Wall and Vallum at Cawfields looking east. Both mounds of the Vallum can be observed, symmetrically placed either side of the ditch*

GILSLAND TO WILLOWFORD

Here is one of the most instructive miles on the whole line of the Wall. This is the only mile where the milecastles at both ends and the two turrets in between can be seen, as well as much of the Wall itself.

At the eastern end sits Poltross Burn milecastle (48). This is larger than usual and it contains two barrack-blocks, one on either side of a central road. The gates are different from those visible at Housesteads and Cawfields milecastles (37 and 42), for example, and suggest that it was built by a different legion, probably the Twentieth. Like several other milecastles, its north gate was narrowed in later years.

Across the railway in the grounds of the former vicarage garden lies the next stretch of Wall. Here the building of the Wall to its original width of 10 Roman feet was never completed and a narrower wall sits on top of a broad base. The modern road has to be crossed to reach the next stretch and from here the Wall runs down to the river Irthing and Willowford bridge. Throughout this

▲ *Willowford Bridge looking east from Harrow's Scar*

▲ *Willowford east turret (48a). The turret was built with wing walls to bond into the broad wall, but by the time the Wall was constructed it had been narrowed and thus, on either side of the turret, there is now a 'point of reduction'*

length, narrow wall usually sits on the uncompleted broad wall. At Poltross Burn milecastle and at the two turrets (48a and 48b) it can be seen that these structures also were completed, with wing walls, at least to their present height, before the Wall was narrowed. At the far end of this sector is Willowford bridge, again built earlier than the narrow wall, though a short length of original broad wall is obscured by a later tower on the south side of the bridge. The river has moved westwards since the Roman period, leaving the bridge on dry land. It also moved during the Roman period and as a result the bridge itself had to be extended westwards. Above the remains of the bridge on the bank of the river sits Harrow's Scar milecastle (49), which is reached from the west.

▶ *Milecastle 48 (Poltross Burn) from the air. Each of the 2 barrack-blocks was originally divided into 4 rooms, perhaps accommodating a total of 32 men*

▼ *The later Hadrianic narrow wall sits uncomfortably on top of the earlier broad wall. Up to five courses of broad wall had been built here before work was temporarily broken off*

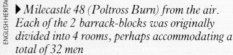

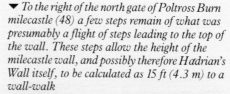

▼ *To the right of the north gate of Poltross Burn milecastle (48) a few steps remain of what was presumably a flight of steps leading to the top of the wall. These steps allow the height of the milecastle wall, and possibly therefore Hadrian's Wall itself, to be calculated as 15 ft (4.3 m) to a wall-walk*

BIRDOSWALD ROMAN FORT

This fort sits on top of the escarpment overlooking the Irthing valley, with splendid views over the valley. To the north the view is more restricted. A road led north from Birdoswald to the outpost fort at Bewcastle.

Most of the circuit of the walls and gates of Birdoswald are in the care of English Heritage: the fort and the surrounding land are owned by Cumbria County Council. Birdoswald lies in the turf sector of Hadrian's Wall and the original fort here may have been of turf and timber, but if so was soon replaced in stone. Like the other forts it was an addition to the Wall. It originally lay astride the turf wall, part of which was demolished to accommodate the fort. Later when the turf wall was rebuilt in stone, the Wall line was moved north so that it met the northern corners of the fort instead of the towers of the main side gates. Birdoswald's garrison under Hadrian is not known, but from the early third century it was the home of the First Aelian Cohort of Dacians (Aelius was Hadrian's family name). This regiment was raised in what is now Romania and, although it will have subsequently recruited from Britain, it continued to display on its altars a symbol of its origin, the curved Dacian sword.

▲ *The east gate of Birdoswald, with its twin entrances, still stands to the height of the first stone of the arch*

▼ *The demolished north granary was replaced by a timber hall rather larger than the granary. The pillars of the hall are marked by modern posts*

▶ *Statue of Fortuna found in the commanding officer's bath-house at Birdoswald*

▼ *Excavations during 1987-89 have revealed the fort's two granaries, probably those whose construction is recorded on an inscription of 205-8. Unusually the granaries had buttresses on one side only. In the late Roman or early post-Roman period the south granary seems to have been re-used as a hall while a large timber building was erected over the north granary. This is the first evidence for complete buildings of such a late date to be found on Hadrian's Wall*

CARLISLE MUSEUM

▲ *This gold ear-ring was found at Birdoswald. It would have been a valuable possession*

DAVID J BREEZE

Tour

The **entrance** in the north wall leads into the **exhibition centre**. To the right lies the **north-west corner** of the fort: here the fort now sits free of Hadrian's Wall, though once it abutted the corner. Inside the corner is a tower containing the remains of two ovens. In front of the former farmhouse lie the **west gate**, **granaries**, a **workshop** or **store**, to the north of which was a hall or **basilica**. Cross the stile and turn right, heading for the **minor west gate**. The inner ditch of the fort survives as a faint hollow and can be traced round the south-west corner of the fort. A few paces from this corner is the edge of the Irthing escarpment.

The **south gate** is visible and along the **east wall** can be seen evidence of successive repairs. The **east gate** is one of the best preserved along the Wall and survives to the top of the pier. Evidence of long use is obvious in the renewal of the gate pivot stones and the modifications to the north tower. Behind the gate lie two window heads. North of the gate is another interval tower.

▲ *West wall and minor west gate at Birdoswald*

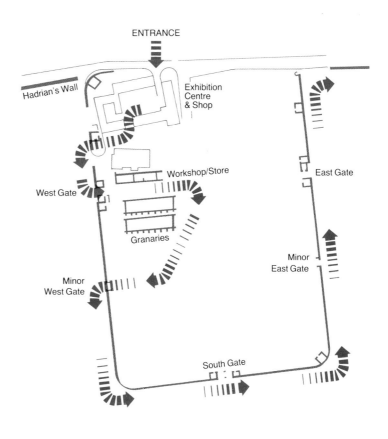

THE TURF WALL

MARYPORT

The whole of the western 30 miles (48 km) of Hadrian's Wall, from the crossing of the river Irthing at Harrow's Scar to Bowness-on-Solway, was originally built of turf. It was probably during Hadrian's reign that a start was made on rebuilding this section of the Wall in stone and the work continued when Hadrian's Wall was reoccupied in the 160s. The first two Roman miles (3.2 km) west of Irthing were replaced on a different line. In places the remains of the turf wall can still be seen running behind the later stone wall.

East of Birdoswald a complete one-third of a Roman mile of Wall stretches to Harrow's Scar milecastle. To the north the ditch is impressive and it is worth walking along the north side to the milecastle and back along the south. In the south face several building stones and phallic symbols (to ward off evil spirits) can still be seen.

To the west of Birdoswald the remains lie beside the modern road. The first turret (49b) is a later (but still Hadrianic) stone wall turret, bonded in with the Wall. The next three turrets were earlier stone towers, built free standing to receive the turf ramparts on either side. On the rise to the east of the last visible turret, 52a (Banks East), lies a fragment of an earlier observation tower, Pike Hill. The troops posted here communicated back to the forts on the Stanegate. The church of Nether Denton, visible a little over 1 mile (2 km) to the left (east) behind the Wall, sits on a Stanegate fort. A short, but tall, length of the Wall can be seen at Hare Hill. One mile along the road to the south-west several Roman stones are on display in the undercroft at Lanercost Priory.

Hadrian's Wall ended at Bowness-on-Solway. Beyond here the coast was protected by forts, milefortlets and towers. Today, little is visible other than the recently laid out fortlet at Swarthy Hill and the well-preserved earthworks of the fort at Maryport 2 miles further south. The fort lies on private land, but may be viewed from the grounds of the adjacent museum.

The fort at Maryport is one of the largest on the frontier at 5.4 acres (2.3 ha). It was probably built under Hadrian for the First Cohort of Spaniards, which was followed in the second century by the First Cohort of Dalmatians and the First Cohort Of Baetasians, a regiment originally raised in the lower Rhineland. The names of the units based here in the third and fourth centuries are not known.

The museum at Maryport, the Senhouse Roman Museum, contains one of the oldest private collections in Britain, having been founded before 1599. It is remarkable for its altars, mostly dedicated to Jupiter, and the depictions of local Celtic gods. These cast a fascinating light on the religious activities of the Roman army.

Twice a year vows were fulfilled for the safety of the emperor over the last year and undertaken for his well-being during the following year: the appropriate sacrifice was an ox. These ceremonies were undertaken on 3 January, two days after every unit in the army had renewed its oath of allegiance to the emperor, and the anniversary of the emperor's accession. Altars may have been erected in a special shrine to Jupiter, the exact location of which north of the fort is now lost.

Maryport appears to possess an almost complete sequence of annual dedications erected by the First Cohort of Spaniards during the reign of Hadrian. These reveal that the average duration of command was three years. The commanders were drawn from Italy, Provence, Noricum (modern Austria), north Africa and possibly Spain. They moved on to posts in the Danubian provinces, Dacia (modern Romania) and Judaea.

▲ A model of a turret on the turf sector of the Wall. There is little evidence to suggest how the top of the turret was completed, and it may have been higher than this model suggests. Archaeogical investigation of turrets has shown that soldiers cooked here

▼ Hadrian's Wall running eastwards from Birdoswald to Harrow's Scar is the longest visible stretch of Wall rebuilt in stone late in Hadrian's reign

▲ A phallic symbol on the south face of the Wall between Harrow's Scar milecastle and Birdoswald fort. This represented good fortune and protection against evil

▼ This stone on the south face of the Wall between Harrow's Scar milecastle and Birdoswald fort records the building of a section of wall by the century of Terentius

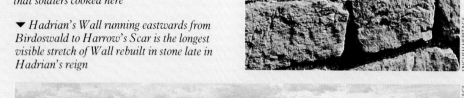

▲ The milefortlet at Swarthy Hill looking west. This is one of a series of milefortlets and towers along the Cumbrian coast: most were abandoned during the second century

◀ The earthworks of the fort at Maryport are clearly visible from the air. Each side contains a gate and beyond the wide rampart lie 2 ditches. The fort is not open to the public but can be viewed from the adjacent museum.

▲ This altar was dedicated to Jupiter by Marcus Maenius Agrippa on behalf of the First Cohort of Spaniards. Agrippa, we know from his career inscription erected at Camerinum in Italy, was a friend of Hadrian and had accompanied the emperor on his visit to Britain. Agrippa was probably the first commander of the newly constructed fort at Maryport in about 123 and may even have entertained Hadrian at Maryport

▲ A horned god, a fertility god with roots deep in prehistory. Maryport was clearly a cult centre as more depictions have been found of this god here than anywhere else in Britain

▲ The 'Serpent Stone' is a large phallic symbol: it takes its name from the serpent which runs up the entire length of one side. On the reverse is a human face framed by two snakes. The stone combines two important symbols, the phallus, a fertility symbol, and the human head, venerated by the Celts as being symbolic of divinity

▲ This badly worn stone is probably the tombstone of a cavalryman based at Maryport

47

CORBRIDGE

This site was occupied longer than any other along the line of Hadrian's Wall. A fort was established here in the 80s and continued in occupation, with one break, into the 160s. Thereafter the nature of the military presence changed. Two compounds were constructed in the southern part of what had been the fort (they were later amalgamated into one), while the granaries were rebuilt and continued in use. Around this military core grew a town which at one time extended to 30 acres (12 ha). The importance of Corbridge sprang from its position at the junction of the Stanegate, which ran westwards to Carlisle,

and Dere Street, leading northwards into Scotland and southward to London. It was also, until the construction of Hadrian's bridge over the Tyne at Newcastle, the lowest crossing-point on the river.

In the centre of the town lay an impressive fountain and a group of temples, which have produced some remarkable sculpture. Gods from the orient as well as local deities were worshipped here. All this reflects the cosmopolitan nature of this town on the very edge of the Roman world.

Also in the heart of the town lies a levelled area on which a large courtyard

building was erected. Construction of this vast building ended abruptly in the late second century, perhaps in the early 180s when the northern tribes are known to have invaded the province. Because it was unfinished it is difficult now to determine its original purpose and suggestions include a storehouse, a legionary headquarters building and the forum for a new town. Within the courtyard lies some remains of the earlier forts, the headquarters building and the commanding officer's house.

Corbridge was occupied until the end of Roman Britain in the early fifth century. It was one of the earliest Roman sites to be 'excavated', for under King John looters came to seek buried treasure. Modern excavation began in 1906 and continued into the 1970s.

◀ *The Corbridge lion. This formerly adorned a fountain in a house south of the military compounds. It was probably originally designed for a tomb*

ENGLISH HERITAGE

▼ *The frieze from a temple showing the sun god riding towards the house of one of the heavenly twins, Castor or Pollux. Such sculptures show how richly ornamented the buildings of Corbridge would have been*

▲ *Bronze jug*

◀ *Pottery lamp*

ENGLISH HERITAGE

▲ *An altar to Jupiter Dolichenus, Caelestis-Brigantia and Salus dedicated by a centurion of legion VI Victrix. This altar illustrates the all-embracing nature of Roman religion. The Roman god Jupiter is identified with the eastern deity Dolichenus, and associated with the personification of the local tribe the Brigantes, who is perceived as a local manifestation of Juno Caelestis, the consort of Jupiter Dolichenus, from either Africa or Syria. The final deity is Salus, the god of personal well-being*

ENGLISH HERITAGE

▲ A sculpture of Hercules killing the Hydra (on the missing piece of the stone), aided by Athena (left). This was found in the central room, the shrine, of the headquarters of the west compound. The god Hercules was particularly favoured by soldiers

ENGLISH HERITAGE

▲ The god Taranis. A plaque made from a pottery mould found at Corbridge

ENGLISH HERITAGE

▼ This depiction of the Sun god probably once adorned a temple to Dolichenus

ENGLISH HERITAGE

Tour

The **museum**, opened in 1983, should be the first stop. On leaving here turn right along the side of the granaries and then left on to the **Stanegate**. This road was in use for over 300 years so it is not surprising that many resurfacings raised its level above the surrounding buildings. The two **granaries** had stone floors supported on low walls. This was to help keep the food dry and fresh. The side vents in the walls were partially closed by mullions: one survives in the east wall of the east granary. A porch over each entrance was supported by the columns on the road side. The right granary retains its loading bay.

Continue along the Stanegate to the **fountain**, with its great water tank in front, fed by an aqueduct, the base for which can be seen leading away behind: a section of the channel survives further north. Below the front of the water tank are the remains of an earlier military building. Walk on to view the great unfinished **courtyard building** (Site XI). Within it lie (left) the headquarters building and (right) the commanding officer's house of an earlier fort. Continue on to the end of the road, passing the remains of **temples** to the right, and turn right to look at the reconstruction drawing of the site. Walk on along the fence and turn right to pass across the site, through the military compounds, passing the officers' houses, to the **headquarters building** of the west compound, in which there is a strong room.

NORTHUMBRIA AIRFOTOS

▲ Corbridge Roman Site. The undulations across the southern (righthand) side of the site are caused by differential subsidence over the roads and buildings of the earlier forts, the roads having prevented subsidence

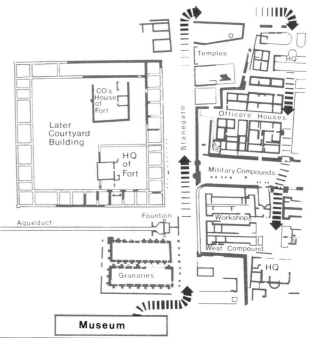

ENGLISH HERITAGE

▲ *A reconstruction of Corbridge as it might have been in the early third century looking west along the Stanegate*

▶ *The east granary looking north. The walls are supported by buttresses; narrow gaps in the walls allowed cool air to enter and circulate below the stone floors of the granaries. The roof was probably originally of tile*

▼ *The only surviving mullion in a granary ventilator slot in Britain is in the east granary at Corbridge*

ENGLISH HERITAGE

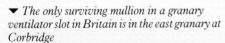

▶ *A view looking along the west side of the unfinished courtyard building, which overlies the remains of the earlier headquarters building. The uncompleted state of the courtyard building is shown by the walls; many stones were only partly dressed by the masons before abandonment. The south range of the building was later converted into shops*

◀ *This base and tank are all that survive of an ornamental fountain, once embellished by statues and sculpture. Behind can be seen the base of the aqueduct which brought water to the fountain*

▼ *The strong room in the headquarters building of the west compound*

RICHARD MUIR

Roman Coinage

Coins were generally in gold, silver and bronze. A gold *aureus* was worth 25 silver *denarii*. A *denarius* was equal to 4 bronze *sestertii*.

Measures of Volume

A Roman *modius* or corn-measure contained sixteen *sextarii*. The modern equivalent of a *sextarius* is a dry-measure pint (568 cc).

Distances

A Roman mile is roughly equivalent to 1620 yd (1479 m). Thus it is smaller than the modern mile of 1760 yd (1609 m). The Roman mile was basically *milia passum* (a thousand paces), a pace (*passus*) being made up of two steps (left and right), resulting in variation. The Roman foot or *pes* has a present equivalent of about 11.6 in (295 mm).

Monument numbering

Milecastles along the course of Hadrian's Wall are numbered from east to west. The sequence starts at Wallsend (0) and ends with Bowness (80). Intervening turrets take the preceding milecastle number, followed by a or b.

Further reading

All the main sites have their own guide-books. A wide range of introductory pamphlets and guide-books are also available at many places along the Wall. The following are more detailed treatments of Hadrian's Wall and its history.

C M Daniels (editor), *Handbook to the Roman Wall*, Newcastle upon Tyne 1978. A comprehensive guide to the frontier system.
D J Breeze and B Dobson, *Hadrian's Wall*, Penguin 1987. A history of Hadrian's Wall and its installations.
Both books provide detailed bibliographies.
R E Birley, *Vindolanda, A Roman frontier post on Hadrian's Wall*, London 1977.
A discussion of the excavations which have taken place at this important site.
R Embleton and F Graham, *Hadrian's Wall in the Days of the Romans*, Newcastle upon Tyne 1984. Important for its reconstruction drawings, which in many cases have to go well beyond the available evidence.
D J Breeze, *The Northern Frontiers of Roman Britain*, London 1982. Attempts to place Hadrian's Wall into its wider British setting.

Recent work is described in:
Charles Daniels (compiler), *The Eleventh Pilgrimage of Hadrian's Wall 26 August-1 September 1989*, Newcastle upon Tyne 1989.

The following consider the history of Roman Britain:

S S Frere, *Britannia*, London 1987
P Salway, *Roman Britain*, Oxford 1981.
R J A Wilson, *A guide to Roman Remains in Britain*, London 1980. An invaluable handbook.

Acknowledgements

The author would like to thank the following for assistance during the preparation of the guidebook: Mr J Barber, Mr P Bidwell, Mr R E Birley, Mr C M Daniels, Mr J Dore, Dr B Dobson, Mr W J Ford, Dr J S Johnson, Miss L Allason-Jones, Professor G D B Jones, Mr J Lang, Mr I MacIvor, Dr Valerie A Maxfield, Mr R Miket, Mr K C Osborne, Mr C Richardson, Dr J Turner, Mr T Wilmott, Dr D Woolliscroft, and the custodians of the English Heritage sites, Mrs M E Rutherford (Chesters), Mr J Robson (Housesteads) and Mr J W Simpson (Corbridge).